Planet Human

T0062290

How Agriculture Changed the World

Stephanie Feldstein

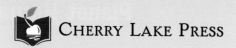
CHERRY LAKE PRESS

Published in the United States of America by Cherry Lake Publishing Group
Ann Arbor, Michigan
www.cherrylakepublishing.com

Reading Adviser: Beth Walker Gambro, MS, Ed., Reading Consultant, Yorkville, IL

Photo Credits: © oticki/Shutterstock; cover, © Don Mammoser/Shutterstock, 4; © Fotokostic/Shutterstock, 5; © Olha Rohulya/Shutterstock, 6; © LaineN/Shutterstock, 9; © Fotokostic/Shutterstock, 10; © Adriano Kirihara/Shutterstock, 11; © bbernard/Shutterstock, 12; © New Africa/Shutterstock, 13; © PeopleImages.com - Yuri A/Shutterstock, 14; © Eugene_Photo/Shutterstock, 15; © Ghinardina/Shutterstock, 16; © oticki/Shutterstock, 17; © Agnieszka Bacal/Shutterstock, 19; © duchy/Shutterstock, 20; © A3pfamily/Shutterstock, 21; © Bilal0833/Shutterstock, 22; © Jerre.Maier/Shutterstock, 25; © PeopleImages.com - Yuri A/Shutterstock, 26; © Rulli Yulianto/Shutterstock, 27; © Nina Firsova/Shutterstock, 28; © Nina Firsova/Shutterstock, 29; © kibler/Shutterstock, 30

Cherry Lake Press is an imprint of Cherry Lake Publishing Group.

Library of Congress Cataloging-in-Publication Data

Names: Feldstein, Stephanie, author.
Title: How agriculture changed the world / written by Stephanie Feldstein.
Description: Ann Arbor, Michigan : Cherry Lake Publishing, [2024] | Series: Planet human | Audience: Grades 4-6 |
    Summary: "The agriculture industry has profoundly impacted our world. The Planet Human series breaks down the human impact on the environment over time and around the globe. Each title presents important high-interest natural science nonfiction content with global relevance"— Provided by publisher.
Identifiers: LCCN 2023035076 | ISBN 9781668939048 (paperback) | ISBN 9781668938003 (hardcover) |
    ISBN 9781668940389 (ebook) | ISBN 9781668941737 (pdf)
Subjects: LCSH: Agriculture—Juvenile literature. | Agriculture—Environmental aspects—Juvenile literature. |
    Agriculture—Health aspects—Juvenile literature. | Agriculture—History—Juvenile literature.
Classification: LCC S519 .F45 2024 | DDC 338.1—dc23/eng/20230906
LC record available at https://lccn.loc.gov/2023035076

Cherry Lake Publishing Group would like to acknowledge the work of the Partnership for 21st Century Learning, a Network of Battelle for Kids. Please visit Battelle for Kids online for more information.

Printed in the United States of America

Stephanie Feldstein works at the Center for Biological Diversity. She advocates to protect wildlife and helps people understand how humans impact nature. She lives in the woods in the Pacific Northwest with her rescued dogs and cats. She loves to hike and explore wild places.

CONTENTS

Introduction

Disappearing Prairies

Prairies might look like overgrown lawns. But lawns are just one type of grass. Prairies have hundreds of different kinds of grasses and wildflowers. Thousands of different kinds of insects live in prairies. More than 300 kinds of birds can be found there. Small mammals like gophers and prairie dogs burrow beneath the grasses. Large mammals like bison and elk graze. Wolves and coyotes hunt there.

Prairies are important for **biodiversity**. They used to cover the middle of the United States. Much of the area is still covered in vast fields of plants. But for many wild animals, it might as well be an empty parking lot. Their food has been replaced by **monocultures**. Monocultures are huge fields with one type of crop. Most are treated with **toxic** chemicals to keep wildlife away.

A Giant Industry

It takes a lot of people to get food from farms to forks. Almost one in three U.S. adults work in food and **agriculture**. They plant and harvest crops. They raise farm animals. They process meat. They cook and serve food. They work in grocery stores.

Almost 37.6 percent of Earth's land is used for agriculture. It uses more land than any other **industry**. Meat and dairy production use the most land. That's because animals need a lot of food. They need much more space than plants. Almost half the land in the lower 48 states is used to raise farm animals.

The meat and dairy industries also use a lot of water. Half of the water used in the United States goes to animal agriculture.

More than half of U.S. prairies are gone. More disappear every year. Most of that land is now used for agriculture. Agriculture is the industry of how people grow crops. It's important for our survival. Crops provide food. They're also used for fuel, clothing, and other products. But industrial agriculture uses practices that harm farmworkers and communities. It harms wildlife and the environment.

Human industry has changed the face of the planet. More than 8 billion people live on Earth. People are living longer. We're healthier than ever. But everything we use or buy comes at a cost. Human industry uses natural resources that wildlife needs. It creates **pollution** and waste. It can affect human health, too. Our industries put a lot of pressure on nature. The most pressure comes from wealthy countries like the United States.

We need a healthy planet to survive. We need clean air and safe water. We need **ecosystems** with lots of different wildlife. Industries like agriculture have a huge impact on the world. But there's a better way. We can farm in ways that are healthier for people and the planet.

CHAPTER 1

The History of Agriculture

About 12,000 years ago, people were hunter-gatherers. They had to move around to find food. Then they figured out how to farm. Crops originally came from wild plants. People chose the best seeds to plant. They also **domesticated** wild animals for meat. They kept the calmest ones. Over time, the wild animals became cows, chickens, and pigs.

Agriculture changed everything. Growing food in one place meant people could settle there. Towns and cities were created. It was easier to feed people. Earth's population grew.

Towns and cities started forming when agriculture made feeding people easier.

By the 1940s, people were worried about world hunger. The growing population needed more food. Scientist Norman Borlaug figured out how to grow more wheat on less land. His ideas sparked the Green Revolution.

The Green Revolution made it easier to grow more food. But it used more water and fertilizer. It used more **pesticides** to keep bugs and weeds from harming crops. It caused more water pollution. It made the soil less healthy.

The new methods also hurt small farmers. Fertilizer and pesticides are expensive. Small farms couldn't afford them. Farms got bigger. But the number of farms shrank. The people planting food made less money. The Green Revolution turned agriculture into a big industry.

Agriculture and Human Health

Pesticides are made to kill living things. They're harmful to people, too. Farmworkers breathe in pesticides sprayed on crops. Almost half of all farmworkers get sick from pesticides. Even people who live near farms can get sick.

Pesticide poisoning can cause rashes and upset stomachs. It can make breathing difficult. It can change how the brain works. It can make pregnant people and babies unhealthy. It can cause cancer and death.

Antibiotics are medicines that fight unhealthy bacteria. Animals raised for food receive 80 percent of all antibiotics produced. Most of these are the same kind needed to treat sick people. But overuse can make antibiotics stop working. This is a big threat to health around the world.

Technology like this harvester has allowed the agriculture industry to grow exponentially.

The industry wanted farming to be the same everywhere. **Indigenous** practices that farmed without harming nature were ignored. People stopped growing traditional foods. They started growing crops that would make more money. But this wasn't always the food they wanted or needed to eat.

Technology helped the agriculture industry keep growing in the 1960s and 1970s. Machines made it easier to plant and harvest crops. New chemicals for fertilizers and pesticides were invented. Scientists decided to create the plants they wanted to grow instead of just choosing the best seeds. They used technology to design crops. This technology is called **genetic engineering**.

People hoped genetic engineering would solve world hunger. But most of these crops were designed to survive pesticides. They weren't designed to be more nutritious. And most of them aren't grown for people to eat. They're grown as food for farm animals.

LEARNING FROM BIOMASS

Biomass measures the weight of plants and animals in an area. It counts the number and size of species. Biomass helps scientists understand ecosystems. Scientists looked at the biomass of all the mammals on Earth. They found that animal agriculture is crowding out wildlife. Humans are 34 percent of the biomass. Farm animals are 62 percent. Wild animals are only 4 percent. Chickens weigh more than twice as much as all wild birds.

The crop most grown to produce animal feed in the United States is corn.

Sometimes, animals at large factory farms
are not given much space to move and grow.

In 2022, farmers planned to plant 91 million acres of soybeans in the United States.

Most farms today grow monocultures. Farm animals are often kept in overcrowded buildings instead of pastures. But people are realizing we need a new Green Revolution. We need to go back to growing lots of different crops. We need to farm in ways that are better for plants and animals.

CHAPTER 2

The Environmental Cost of Agriculture

Agriculture is the greatest threat to biodiversity. Wild plants and animals need **habitat** to survive. Habitat is wildlife's natural home. More than 18 million acres (7.2 million hectares) of forests are turned into farms or pastures each year. That's as big as 27 soccer fields disappearing every minute. Grasslands are also turned into farms and pastures. U.S. grasslands are in danger of disappearing.

Pesticides are made to poison wildlife. They're meant for wild plants and animals that might harm crops. But they make other wildlife sick, too. Pesticides harm birds.

Insecticides and weed killers can kill songbirds like the ruby-throated hummingbird.

Manure produced by farm animals can fertilize crops, but it can also pollute rivers.

They kill bugs that make soil healthy. Pesticides from fields wash into streams. They make the water toxic for fish and amphibians. Pesticides also kill **native plants** that wildlife eat. Then the animals don't have enough food.

Farm animals create 500 million tons of manure a year. The waste washes into rivers. It's polluted more than 35,000 miles (56,327 kilometers) of U.S. rivers.

Changemaker: Rowen White

Rowen White fell in love with seeds as a teenager. She realized seeds told a story. They told her what her ancestors ate. They connected her to her Mohawk community. They helped her understand what it means to be human. She calls seeds "a beautiful living bridge between yesterday and tomorrow."

Once many types of seeds existed. But 94 percent of seed types have disappeared during the past 100 years. Agriculture needs diversity. Diversity protects against crop diseases. It grows healthier food.

White is a seed keeper. She leads an organization called Sierra Seeds. It educates the community about seeds. White helped create the Indigenous Seed Keepers Network. The network supports Indigenous communities growing traditional foods. It teaches people about the importance of seeds.

Pollinators like bees are needed to pollinate flowering crops like these almond trees.

The agriculture industry destroys ecosystems. It makes **climate change** worse. But agriculture needs a healthy environment. Reducing climate change makes it easier to farm. Planting different kinds of crops keeps soil healthy. Saving bees and butterflies helps crops grow. We can change how we grow food to protect nature. And that will help us keep growing enough food.

SAY NO TO FOOD WASTE

Almost 40 percent of food in the United States is wasted. That's like throwing two of every five bites in the garbage. Uneaten food is the biggest source of trash in landfills. This waste creates more of the gas methane. More methane in the atmosphere makes global warming worse. It's dangerous for wildlife.

Uneaten food also wastes everything that went into growing the food. Stopping food waste would save land and water. It would help protect wildlife. It would make sustainable agriculture easier.

CHAPTER 3

Roots of Change

The Green Revolution made it easier to grow food. But it backfired. The industry got too big. Pesticides are killing bees, butterflies, and other wildlife that help farmers. Climate change makes it harder to grow crops. Animal agriculture is drying up water sources.

Many people are worried about the problems caused by the agriculture industry. They're trying to go back to less harmful practices. **Agroecology** is a way of farming sustainably without monocultures. It works with nature. It avoids using toxic chemicals. It takes care of the soil. It protects biodiversity.

Agroecology also supports people. The agriculture industry is controlled by big companies. But agroecology involves farmworkers. People share traditional knowledge.

Ensuring the soil is healthy is one of the main tenets of agroecology.

Community-supported agriculture (CSA) allows farms to sell directly to consumers. According to the United States Department of Agriculture, over a quarter of CSAs are organic.

Agroecology has been around a long time. It's used by many Indigenous farmers. It's used by small farmers around the world. And it's a way to make agriculture better for people and the planet.

Many big agriculture companies don't want to change. They make a lot of money by using often harmful practices. They don't have to pay for the pollution they cause. They may not worry about the future of farming. But people are demanding change. They're asking companies to grow food differently. They want companies

We can't just change how we grow food. We also need to change what we grow and eat. People in the United States eat more meat than most other countries. Beef is 20 times worse for the climate than beans. It uses 20 times more land. Chicken, pork, and dairy also use more resources.

CLIMATE-FRIENDLY FOOD

Scientists say we have to change what we eat to fight climate change. Foods like beef that come from animals create a lot of climate pollution. Foods like beans that come from plants create very little pollution.

Cities around the world are starting to include food in their climate action. They're making menus more climate friendly. Cities buy a lot of food. They buy food for schools. They buy food for hospitals and other places. These cities are serving more plant-based foods. They're buying less meat. The new menus will help cities meet their climate goals.

The Future of Agriculture

The meat and dairy industries are tough on the planet. But they're a big part of people's diets. Americans eat about 50 billion hamburgers a year. It's hard for people to give up foods they love. So scientists are creating meat without animals. It has less of an impact on the planet.

The newest plant-based burgers are made to taste like beef. Scientists even try to mimic the cell structure of beef. This makes the burgers look and cook like beef. Companies are working to make other types of meat from plants, too.

Cultivated meat is made from animals. But no animals are killed to make it. Scientists only need animal cells. Then they grow the meat from those cells.

There are so many plant-based meals to try! Have fun experimenting in the kitchen.

Replacing meat and dairy with plant foods helps the environment. It uses less land and water. It's better for the climate and wildlife. It's better for our health, too. Restaurants are adding more plant choices to their menus. Schools are serving meatless meals. This makes it easier for people to eat planet-friendly food. It supports farmers

Activity

Plan a Sustainable Dinner

Our food choices help farmers decide what to grow. It helps grocery stores decide what to keep on their shelves. We can create demand for sustainable food at every meal.

Start by planning a sustainable dinner:

1. **Choose plant power.** The first step is deciding what to make. Choosing a plant-based recipe will have the biggest impact.

2. **Think local.** Next, you have to shop for ingredients. Most vegetables in grocery stores are shipped from far away. They're grown on industrial farms. Find out if you have a farmer's market near you instead.

3. **Go organic.** Try to choose organic ingredients. Look for the organic label in stores. At the farmer's market, ask if they use pesticides.

4. **Use everything.** Think about how you'll avoid wasting any food. Think about how you can use extra ingredients for another meal. Plan for when you'll eat any leftovers.

5. **Plan the next sustainable meal.** Talk with your family about the dinner. What did they like about it? Were there things they didn't like? How can you start making all your meals more sustainable?

Learn More

Books

Feldstein, Stephanie. *Save Pollinators.* Ann Arbor, MI: Cherry Lake Publishing, 2023.

Gigliotti, Jim. *Who Was George Washington Carver?* New York, NY: Penguin Workshop, 2015.

Knutson, Julie. *Garden to Table.* Ann Arbor, MI: Cherry Lake Publishing, 2019.

Veness, Kimberley. *Let's Eat!: Sustainable Food for a Hungry Planet.* Victoria, BC: Orca Book Publishers, 2017.

On the Web

With an adult, learn more online with these suggested searches.

"10 Food Waste Facts for Kids" — Earth.org

"What Is Climate Change?" — *National Geographic Kids*

"World Biomes: Grassland" — *Kids Do Ecology, National Geographic Society*

Glossary

agriculture (AG-rih-kuhl-chuhr) the industry of how people grow crops

agroecology (AG-roh-ee-KAH-luh-jee) sustainable farming that works with nature

antibiotics (an-tye-bye-AH-tiks) medicines that fight bacteria that make people or animals sick

biodiversity (bye-oh-duh-VUHR-suh-tee) the variety of plants and animals in nature

biomass (BYE-oh-mas) the weight of plants and animals in an area

climate change (KLYE-muht CHAYNJ) changes in weather, temperatures, and other natural conditions over time

domesticated (duh-MEH-stih-kayt-id) the state of becoming tame

ecosystems (EE-koh-sih-stuhmz) places where plants, animals, and the environment rely on each other

genetic engineering (jeh-NEH-tik en-juh-NEER-ing) a scientific process that changes the inherited traits of a plant or animal

habitat (HAB-uh-tat) the natural home of plants and animals

Indigenous (in-DIH-juh-nuhs) the culture, traditions, and knowledge of the first people who lived in a region

industry (IN-duh-stree) all the companies that make and sell a kind of product or service

monocultures (MAH-nuh-kuhl-chuhrz) huge fields with one type of crop

native plants (NAY-tiv PLANTS) plants that are a natural part of an ecosystem

organic (or-GAN-ik) food or other plants grown without toxic chemicals

pesticides (PEH-stuh-siedz) toxic chemicals made to kill a plant or animal that might harm crops

pollution (puh-LOO-shuhn) harmful materials released into the environment

toxic (TAHK-sik) something that is harmful or poisonous

Index